The Colors We Eat

Yellow Foods

Patricia Whitehouse

Heinemann Library
Chicago, Illinois

Customer Service 888-454-2279
Visit our website at www.heinemannlibrary.com

Designed by Sue Emerson, Heinemann Library
Printed and bound in the U.S.A. by Lake Book

06 05 04 03 02
10 9 8 7 6 5 4 3 2 1

Library of Congress Cataloging-in-Publication Data
Whitehouse, Patricia, 1958-
   Yellow foods / Patricia Whitehouse.
       p. cm. — (The colors we eat)
Includes index.
Summary: Introduces things to eat and drink that are yellow, from pineapples to apple cider.
   ISBN: 1-58810-537-7 (HC), 1-58810-745-0 (Pbk.)
   1. Food—Juvenile literature. 2. Yellow—Juvenile literature. [1. Food. 2. Yellow.] I. Title.
   TX355 .W49 2002
   641.3—dc21
                   2001004797

Acknowledgments
The author and publishers are grateful to the following for permission to reproduce copyright material:
Title page, p. 11 Phil Degginger; pp. 4, 5, 8, 17 Michael Brosilow/Heinemann Library; pp. 6, 18, 19 Greg Beck/Fraser Photos; pp. 7, 13, 16L Rick Wetherbee; p. 9 AgStock USA; p. 10 Inga Spence/Visuals Unlimited; pp. 12, 16R Amor Montes de Oca; p. 14 Bill Beatty; p. 15 Ed Young/AgStock USA; pp. 20, 21L, 21R Craig Mitchelldyer Photography

Cover photograph by Michael Brosilow/Heinemann Library

Every effort has been made to contact copyright holders of any material reproduced in this book. Any omissions will be rectified in subsequent printings if notice is given to the publisher.

Special thanks to our advisory panel for their help in the preparation of this book:
Eileen Day, Preschool Teacher
Chicago, IL

Paula Fischer, K–1 Teacher
Indianapolis, IN

Sandra Gilbert,
Library Media Specialist
Houston, TX

Angela Leeper,
Educational Consultant
North Carolina Department
of Public Instruction
Raleigh, NC

Pam McDonald, Reading Teacher
Winter Springs, FL

Melinda Murphy,
Library Media Specialist
Houston, TX

Helen Rosenberg, MLS
Chicago, IL

Anna Marie Varakin,
Reading Instructor
Western Maryland College

Some words are shown in bold, **like this.**
You can find them in the picture glossary on page 23.

Contents

Have You Eaten Yellow Foods?

Colors are all around you.

You might have eaten some of these colors.

There are yellow fruits and vegetables.

There are other yellow foods, too.

What Are Some Big Yellow Foods?

Pineapples are big and yellow.

Pineapple plants have long, sharp leaves.

These melons are big and yellow.

Melons grow on long **vines.**

What Are Some Other Big Yellow Foods?

This **squash** is big and yellow.

The inside looks like spaghetti noodles!

This grapefruit is big and yellow.

Grapefruits grow on trees.

What Are Some Small Yellow Foods?

Lemons are small and yellow.

Lemons grow on trees.

Star fruits are small and yellow.

When you cut them, they look like stars.

What Are Some Other Small Yellow Foods?

Chickpeas are small and yellow.

People cook chickpeas before they eat them.

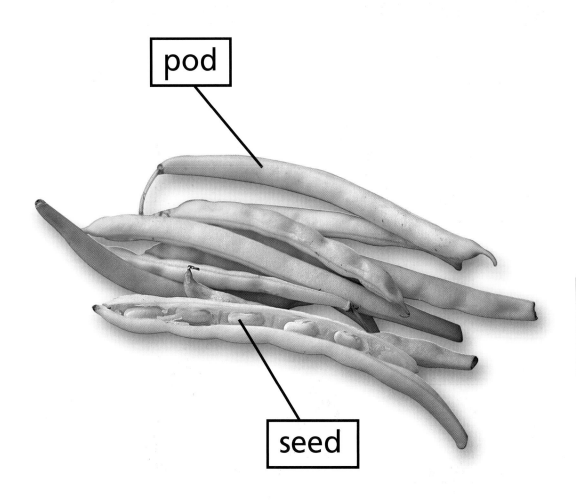

pod

seed

Wax beans are small and yellow.

Wax beans are the **pod** and the seeds inside it.

What Are Some Crunchy Yellow Foods?

Corn is crunchy and yellow.

Kernels of corn grow on corncobs.

This **pepper** is crunchy and yellow.

Yellow peppers grow on plants.

What Are Some Soft Yellow Foods?

Bananas are soft and yellow.

Bananas grow on tall **stems.**

Butter is soft and yellow.

Butter is made from milk.

What Yellow Foods Can You Drink?

Lemonade is a yellow drink.

It is made by squeezing the juice out of lemons.

Apple cider is a yellow drink.

It is made by pressing the juice out of apples.

Yellow Fruit Kabob Recipe

Ask an adult to help you.

Cut some **pineapple,** bananas, and **star fruit** into pieces.

Next, push some pieces of fruit onto a toothpick.

Then eat your yellow fruit **kabob!**

Quiz

Can you name these foods?

Look for the answers on page 24.

Picture Glossary

 **chickpeas**
page 12

 **pod**
page 13

 **kabob**
page 20–21

 **squash**
page 8

 **kernels**
page 14

 **star fruit**
page 11, 20

 **pepper**
page 15

 **stem**
page 16

 **pineapple**
pages 6, 20

 **vine**
page 7

Note to Parents and Teachers

Reading for information is an important part of a child's literacy development. Learning begins with a question about something. Help children think of themselves as investigators and researchers by encouraging their questions about the world around them. Each chapter in this book begins with a question. Read the question together. Look at the pictures. Talk about what you think the answer might be. Then read the text to find out if your predictions were correct. Think of other questions you could ask about the topic, and discuss where you might find the answers. Assist children in using the picture glossary and the index to practice new vocabulary and research skills.

Index

Answers to quiz on page 22

pepper · lemon · bananas · lemonade · pineapple · squash · melon · onion · butter · pear · corn · grapefruit · kiwano · tomatoes